Modelling Community Mission

Closing the Gap between Church and Community

Rev Dr Stephen J Cave

Kingdom Publishers

Copyright© Rev Dr Stephen J Cave 2025

All rights reserved. No part of this book may be reproduced in any form by photocopying or any electronic or mechanical means, including information storage or retrieval systems, without permission in writing from both the copyright owner and the publisher of the book. The right of Rev Dr Stephen J Cave to be identified as the author of this work has been asserted by him in accordance with the Copyright, Designs, and Patents Act 1988 and any subsequent amendments thereto.

A catalogue record for this book is available from the British Library.

All Scripture quotations have been taken from the New International version of the Bible.

ISBN: 978-1-916801-32-5

1st Edition 2025 by Kingdom Publishers, London, UK.

You can purchase copies of this book from any leading bookstore or at:
www.kingdompublishers.co.uk

Dedication

In memory of Michael and Val Jones. We laughed a lot, cried a little and ate far too much chicken together. You mended our broken wings and taught us how to fly again.

The story that is told here (without a single embellishment) is dedicated to: -

All my friends at Queens Road Baptist Church, Broadstairs (both past and present) who had the grace to tolerate my endless pursuit of the 'better'

All the amazing people who over 30 years helped to make the Gap Project what it is today

To Gill Corker Project Manager without whom there would be no story. "Sometimes 'gold-dust' stands in the doorway to an office." A true and honest friend, much loved and always first to buy a round of drinks for the staff.

To Rev. Samuel Hearle. Who apart from his annoying habit of calling me 'matey' (like something you put in a bath) has proven to be the kindest and most gracious person anyone could hope to work alongside and never gave up on me even when he knew I was well out of line.

Contents

Introduction	9
Chapter 1 – "To the ends of the earth"	13
Chapter 2 – Closing the Gap	20
Chapter 3 – Standing in the Gap	30
Chapter 4 – A Charitable Enterprise	37
Chapter 5 – A new building	47
Recommended Reading	51

Introduction

This is a book about one church based in the Southeast of England, principally in the District of Thanet, specifically the town of Broadstairs and precisely Queens Road and its desire to model, "Community Mission".

Now that's what I call an opening sentence. If you don't like it don't give up. It will feature several times. Just ignore it. If it annoys you just use a thick black marker pen to cover it up. If you are reading this on a device don't. Be sure to look up Broadstairs on the internet if you have no idea where that is - neither did I before coming to live here – more of that later.

It is written by someone who was one of the Ministers at the church for nearly30 years and will of course mostly reflect my own perspective. I'm sure there will be a few who would want to issue the disclaimer – "the views here do not necessary reflect the views of the management" – so apologies in advance if that is the case. Hopefully it will be honest – warts and all.

The story will draw on the inspiration that ensued from many of those who were 'key' to the adventure of engaging in community mission, although I recognise everyone played a part – an 'adventure' I hasten to add continues and thrives. I have had the privilege of sharing life with so many people here at this church, people who have inspired me, challenged, and guided me. Some of them still send Christmas cards. Without them there would be no story. If Community Mission is anything it's a team game. The clue is in the name.

The reader will hear something of this story, can reflect on some of the theology that under-pinned it, and view the way that theology was applied and practiced for better and worse. Hopefully all told with 'humour' and grace and without any assumption that this is how church is best done. Every church has its own individual thumb print and must find out how that might look but we can learn from each other – mistakes and all. Mostly we learn best from the mistakes of others. There will be plenty to learn from in this story.

Having looked at four models of church in my doctrinal thesis I am aware there are as many ways of 'doing church' and 'being church' as there are Christian conferences. Maybe not quite as many as Church conferences but check out the four models I wrote about if you have nothing better to do with your time[1]. It's proved to be so popular that Amazon are now giving it away free with every delivery of Marmite and like Marmite it divides opinion. It was meant to.

The model of community mission I am reflecting on in this book has been particularly influenced by the writing of two practitioners, Ann Morisy and John Reader. Ann Morisy was a freelance community theologian and lecturer, and she directed the commission that produced the report 'Faithful Cities'[2] for the Anglican Church. Her best-known book is *Beyond the Good Samaritan*[3], which later she expanded and developed in *Journeying Out*[4]. John Reader was the Priest-In-Charge of the Four-Square Parishes and associate Training and Educational Officer, for the Diocese of Worcester. In 1994 he wrote *Local Theology*[5]. Although dated, these books, together with so many others brilliant books written by theologians and practitioners (which I will list at the end of the book) provided a theological backdrop to what emerged in the church I was called to.

"And to the ends of the earth[6]," He declared. So, in my ill-informed and geographical naivete I heard His call to the Southeast of England, principally in the District of Thanet, specifically the town of Broadstairs and precisely Queens Road Baptist Church. Ignited by "Community Mission" I headed for a

---

1 Available from Amazon as an e-book titled "Faith, Politics and Spirituality – 4 models of practice for Church engagement" Rev Dr Stephen Cave
2 http://www.cofe.anglican.org/search?SearchableText=Faithful+Cities&go=Go
3 Ann Morisy, Beyond the Good Samaritan, Mowbray 1997
4 Ann Morisy, Journeying Out, Morehouse 2004
5 John Reader, Local Theology, SPCK 1994
6 Acts 1:8 - NIV

church already ignited by "Community Mindedness". When I got there, they were re-painting the outside doors 'blue' and painting over 'red'. If it was a political statement, I was in trouble. It wasn't.

Chapter 1 – "To the ends of the earth"

It was time to move on from the church I was at in Bristol and so I went on the 'list' which at that time meant that every month you received a 'list' of churches looking for someone with your 'gifting' and focus. Following this you then wait for them to get in touch and go from there. By the time my second monthly list arrived I was increasingly becoming aware that my geographical knowledge was somewhat limited. Either that or I was not in great demand from places with a population over 52 and churches with anyone under the age of 75. I hardly knew where any of the listed churches were.

I had a few sparks of interest which soon went out when they discovered that I still liked to wear a baseball hat and the occasional hoodie. Then came the phone-call from Broadstairs. "Yes, I would love to come down to preach with a 'squint' and to meet with the Deacons". I would have to practice my 'squint', but I was up for it. "By the way where is Broadstairs?"

Having spent 7 years living in Pembrokeshire I should have been prepared for the journey to Broadstairs. I think I assumed that the Southeast came to an end once you had crawled your way around the M25. I was wrong – 2 hours wrong. At the time there was no Thanet Way (the highway that leads you to the promised land), just a route that took you around the houses. Sometimes through them. "To the ends of the earth" He said. It felt like it. Mind you the 'scales fell from my eyes' (inserted to help me squint) when I saw Broadstairs. If I had to learn to 'squint' to live in this beautiful town then squint, I would.

Having 'squinted' and 'viewed'[7] the church and been invited to join them on their 'adventure' we re-located and started to get to know people and what it was that made the church what it already was. And what it was is 'community minded'. The existing Minister who I was called to work alongside was open

---

[7] At this time prospective Ministers were often asked to preach firstly with a 'squint' and then with a 'view'. How quaint is that.

hearted and open handed and was pure joy to work with and already the church had several activities which connected with the wider community. There were visions and dreams in the pipeline for more community involvement and there was an openness to discover how that might look. What I saw as my task was to help the church to develop what already existed and to 'formalise' that in some way. In other words, to move on from the position of 'community mindedness' to 'community mission'.

At the time it was Morisy and Reader who helped me to focus on the significance of community mission and shaped much of my thinking in those early days at the church. I even got the Deacons to get a copy of "Journeying beyond the Good Samaritan". Some of them might even have read it. I know of one that did and soon they were at the forefront of community mission through the Project we went on to establish. I like to think it was down to the book I suggested, others see it as down to God. I leave you to decide. I was invoiced by the church at the end of the month for 8 copies which I have more than settled for through the inordinate number of biscuits I have had to ply people with over the last 25 years (more on that subject later). Just for legal reasons the church didn't invoice me.

I was immediately struck by the way Morisy suggests that community mission enabled people, "to gain new ways of seeing and understanding"[8] and to "embrace a struggle wider than themselves"[9]. Having grown up in an Evangelical setting I was intrigued by writers who were openly asking questions about what 'conversion' – that is a 'new way of seeing and understanding' – is, and how and where it might take place. What I was discovering (having the opportunity to think about) was that my own understanding of 'conversion' was being challenged. Not only challenged but widened – 'embracing a struggle wider than themselves' - a largely missing element in Evangelical churches due to the stress on 'personal conversion' as a reflection of individuality rather than mutuality. Morisy seemed to me, to be

---

8 Ann Morisy, Beyond the Good Samaritan, Mowbray 1997 p. x
9 Ibid p. 25

suggesting something that needed to be taken on board, if community mission was to be, well, community mission.

Hanging around the walls of theological education at Spurgeon's College in London[10] as I was at that time, I could see that Morisy was taking the concept of 'conversion' beyond the more traditional view you find for example in books written by the American activist Jim Wallis, (another influential thinker in my journey). Wallis, in my opinion, tends to limit his understanding of community as a "place of conversion"[11] to the Christian community (however that is expressed). I guess in the Christian world he is not alone in that. Conversion is often associated with church – an in-house experience rather than an out-of- house, one. What I liked about Morisy and Reader is that in their view community mission extends beyond it in its provision for people outside the Christian community and offered the possibility of conversion outside of the confines of the church. I'm sure many of my Catholic brothers and Sisters would baulk at that. All respect to them. However, I couldn't settle with Wallis' view of conversion taking place within the community of faith[12] alone. I also wasn't in complete agreement with Morisy when she argues for a primary focus on the potential for conversion in the wider community[13]. I guess there is no pleasing some people. Having spent most of my life sitting on the fence (a somewhat painful experience) I have no intention of climbing down on one side or another. It's a classic case of not 'either' but 'both'. If St. Paul can be converted on the road to Damascus and John Wesley in a Christian gathering that's good enough for me. Meeting Jesus is not dependant on location, its dependant on, well, meeting Jesus.

It seems to me that the term 'conversion' carries with it an assumption that everyone is talking about the same kind of experience but clearly it can have all

---

10 A great place to work through some ideas in a warm and embracing environment. Thoroughly recommend it. No doubt like all centres of education at the moment they could do with your fees. Go on take out a student loan. You will never have to pay in back if you stay in Christian ministry!
11 Jim Wallis, The Call to Conversion, Lion Paperback 1981 p. 123
12 Jim Wallis, The Soul of Politics, Orbis Books 1994 p. 184
13 Ann Morisy, Beyond the Good Samaritan, Mowbray 1997 p. 15

kinds of different understandings. I think what Morisy and others were talking about is the kind of conversion that David Augsburger[14] defines as "tripolar spirituality"[15]; a conversion which embraces personal transformation, Divine encounter, and solidarity with our neighbour. In my view this is the kind of conversion that community mission encourages and again in my view is a more complete conversion. It's both an inward and outward, individual and corporate, the bringing together of people from the community of faith with people who at this stage would not place themselves in that grouping which can enable 'conversion' in its widest terms. Hence the view held by many of the thinkers and activists that I have engaged with over the years that conversion is both individual and corporate. A personal moment set in a communal context. Hence for Morisy conversion is not limited to those who would identify themselves as being part of a Christian community. Startling I know, even controversial, but like a good wine give it some air and time to mature. If it still tastes corked, then other methodologies of mission are available which I'm sure are just as good.

Reader sees that it is in the dialogue between the Christian community and the wider community[16] that mutual conversion can take place If Community Mission is anything its clearly about two communities talking, learning and engaging together. Seldom, in my view do people within the church realise how much they will be changed through genuine and not-one-sided conversations and activities with people from outside the Christian community. Community mission is not about doing stuff for others – a facet so loved by 'servant' faith communities - it's about doing things together. If you want to stay the same, or even want the church to stay the same, then I would suggest avoiding community mission. Working with the homeless, the lonely, the one's struggling emotionally, socially, economically or mentally will change you. In fact, you may well realise for the first time the incredible mutuality between you and them. So much so that the language changes to 'us'. Morisy describes

---

14 David Augsburger, Dissident Discipleship, Brazos Press 2006
15 Ibid p. 13
16 John Reader, Local Theology, SPCK 1994 pp. 83-86

this place of mutual conversion as "adaptive zones"[17]. In this adaptive zone - the place of dialogue and potential conversion – as she sees it. there is no attempt to clone people from the wider community into the image of the Christian community. Nor does the Christian community want to become cloned in the image of the wider community, in other words arrive at the place Reader describes as 'false commonality'[18]. Instead Morisy presents a vision of a reformed community in its widest sense, which is both church and community experiencing conversion through genuine dialogue[19]. I think Morisy is right to stress the importance of the local church having the confidence and security to engage in dialogue[20] with the wider community, because none of us realised at the outset how much we would be changed. I didn't – you won't. I'll leave the last word to Donal Dorr.

"To 'opt for the poor' it is not enough for me to be providing services for them; I must be in some way with them, sharing at least some of their experiences, suffering and hoping with them. Together we may be able to work for a more just and human society, starting from below rather than from above"[21].

Having struggled through 'treacle' (theological debate – same thing) in the last few paragraphs, hopefully some thoughts to get us thinking, let me take you back to the adventure that we were on. Initially that involved inviting people to become part of a 'mission think-tank'. I love a bit of jargon and that is a classic example of it. Forget the title it proved to be a worthwhile place to start. The group members came from all kinds of different places. Some had a more traditional view of evangelism from organised mission events to secreting 'tracts[22],' in people's food. Added to that 'let's have more Bible verses so that when people come into the halls, they can be challenged by Scripture' was forwarded. In the end we agreed that maybe we needed to be a 'letter from

---

17 Ann Morisy, Journeying Out, Morehouse 2004 p. 22
18 John Reader, Local Theology, SPCK 1994 p. 91
19 Donal Dorr, Spirituality and Justice, Gill and McMillan 1984 p. 84
20 Ann Morisy, Beyond the Good Samaritan, Mowbray 1997 p. 66
21 Ibid p. 17
22 Little booklets of dubious quality that basically tell people how bad they are and where bad people end up

Christ[23],' ourselves. If people were going to read anything it had to be us as disciples of Jesus. We just had to find a way of letting them in on that. Others thought about an annual mission – maybe invite a gifted Evangelist and invite family and friends from the community to it. We all knew that none of us would really want to do that and that even if we did no-one would come. Acting on 'guilty feelings' and 'we ought to be doing this, but we bulk at the thought' was old school and together we realised that we had to be courageous and start to think in new ways. Thankfully no-one mentioned 'knocking on doors' to carry out meaningless questionnaires as a cunning method of opening conversations. Leave that to the professionals I suggest. There are plenty out there. You know them by their limp which is caused by people constantly slamming the door on a foot that was strategically placed in their doorway.

It was an exciting start, and we were all being 'converted[24],' towards a new understanding of community mission. Without this kind of conversation and a willingness to hear each other, people, I would suggest, will never get onboard and will in the end gladly, and much to their relief, stand back and watch you getting on. Of course, they will be 'right behind you' and I mean right behind you. As one Headmaster once told me "If you are one step ahead of people they will follow – if two or three steps ahead they will let you carry on". Sound advice I think so I tried not to short-circuit these conversations and learnt to value them as we 'adventured together'. We may have read all the books, attended all the conferences, they have done life and have experiences that are essential to the journey ahead. It is 'community mission'.

These conversations got us started the outcome of which was to begin to think in terms of a social project. A project that would bring some of the existing community activities and create new ones that would formalise and shape future involvement. Some of those who had been there from the start stepped back – not in a negative way – and new voices emerged. Many of those now coming on board had experience of how a social project might be brought about and their expertise would prove invaluable. I like to see the different

---

23 2 Corinthians 3:2-3 - NIV
24 Jim Wallis, The Call to Conversion, Lion Paperback 1981 p. 123

stages you go through in developing a project as being like a relay-race where the baton is passed on from one runner who has covered their distance to the next. Same race different runners. And from a relay-race you soon learn not to hold on to the baton for too long or else the next athlete cannot run their course. Which included me when the time came.

Thankfully no one was being 'precious' about holding onto the baton. It's always going to be a problem in any organisation - and I think the church can be prone to this - when someone hangs on to the baton for too long. It tends to suffocate progress. Maybe suggest they see their doctor to arrange for the baton to be surgically removed or arrange for some of the characters that you are intending to work with to mug them and run off with it. Perhaps follow what Ezra the priest did before the disobedient and unwilling people following the restoration of Jerusalem[25]. That would shock them so much they would drop the baton. Dealing with it, as you must for it cannot be ignored, in a pastorally sensitive way can be a challenge but grace will always prove sufficient[26]. I have the scars to prove it. I think it amazing how people connect with and contribute to a journey like this at various stages. Some might return later; many will move on to other opportunities that the church and wider community provide. Everyone needs to be valued for the part they have played, continue to play or will in some future date join in. And an amazing number of people have played their part over the years and without them little or nothing would have happened.

---

25 Ezra 9:3-4 NIV
26 2 Corinthians 12:9 NIV

Chapter 2 – Closing the Gap

In my opinion (and I have a lot of them) there are some people of faith who have very jaundiced view of those who don't share, or remain uncertain, about their faith. How many times have you heard people from the church refer to people out in the wider community as having a 'sad life' or worse? Basically, that is because a lot of us have buried ourselves underneath church-based activities that we know very few, if anyone, from the wider community. Not in any meaningful way. It's a biological fact that no-one has a 'G-shaped hole' in their heart that only God can fill, nor (mostly) are they spending their lives searching for the 'missing piece'[27]. As far as I can see they are just getting on with life and mostly feel comfortable with that. We all face difficult times in life and to be honest (in my view) seem to manage as well, if not better at times, with the struggles. Maybe it's just that they have no Divine expectations and that gives them a sense that this is just how life is. They have no-one to feel let down by or need to create some 'wiggle room' in their theology of suffering that doesn't hold up in the dark times. Ouch, that's going to be controversial. The point is that we will never reach beyond ourselves based on assumptions.

What we might assume any community needs or people might lack, second guessing doesn't help. Added to that there is little point in a church trying to duplicate what others are already doing. They are often better resourced and better trained. Community mission is about partnership. It's not about the church doing its own thing regardless of what other community groups and charities are doing and trying to muscle in. If anything, it's about spotting the gaps that exist and working alongside others to see how best the church can contribute. That is not to deny that the church has something distinctive to bring just that the distinctive works best alongside others, else how will people see the differences?

---

27 Both terms are often used in evangelism.

The outcome of this for us was to carry out a community audit. There are other ways of going about this too. Given the technological advancements that have taken place since 1999-2000 I'm sure a better methodology is available. For us it was about researching what was already being provided and assessing where the gaps remained. Talking to people outside the church with their finger on the beating pulse of the community was so helpful. Everyone was so positive and seemed to be so pleased that we were looking to get involved in a district that at that time was among the most deprived in the country[28]. There was no shortage of needs – where is there? And in Thanet that remains the case. Marginalisation seeps through the structures in most areas. Getting to grips with that and trying to understand what that meant and how we were going to respond was quite the task. It seems to be in vogue in the political world to claim to have come from a working family that experienced marginalisation which is difficult to authenticate when you are wearing a £500 suit with designer accessories (Must get that "plank" out of my eye[29]). Maybe we do some of that in church too. Maybe I have done some of that. Its best to just be who you are and where you have come from and find positive ways to stand alongside those who have not be dealt a fair hand in life.

In her book *'Mission on the Margins'*, Mary Beasley defines the term marginal as "those who fall outside the social structures"[30]. Later she further develops the term by drawing on Minjung Theology as, "those who are oppressed politically, exploited economically, alienated sociologically, and kept uneducated in cultural and intellectual matters"[31]. I don't think all of that is necessarily true, but I got the picture. To be honest you can see it for yourself. Hang out around the local town centre for a few hours or hop on a local bus or stand outside the council offices and benefit offices. It's not rocket science. You would need to blindfold not to see how people are struggling. See the 17-

---

28 As measured by the 2007 national indices of deprivation Thanet is the 65th (out of 354) most deprived district in England. Within the District there are pockets of severe deprivation including the two most deprived wards in the whole South East of England (Margate Central and Cliftonville West). – Thanet District Council Webpage
29 Matthew 7:3-5 (NIV)
30 Mary Beasley, Ministry on the Margins, The Lutterworth Press 1997 p. 10
31 Ibid p. 54

year-old single mum pushing the pram through the town centre trying to be the best mum she can but struggling to make ends meet and support her much loved newborn. Hear the shouts of torment and confusion from the guy struggling with mental health issues alone and unsupported. Watch the lonely figure of the asylum seeker confused and a long way from the world they have grown up in and facing the stares that suggest a less than welcoming community. Spot the teenager taking the long way home because what waits at home is worse than anyone could imagine. Community Mission I believe enables the church to take off that blindfold and to see not just the despair but the possibilities. That's what Morisy helped us to see – possibilities.

Seeing and getting hold of the possibilities creates opportunities for what Morisy defines as "Kingdom reversals"[32], reversals which, as described by Augsburger; enable slaves to be set free, resources shared, redistributive policies to be put on the statute books, enemies loved, outsiders to become insiders, values to be transformed, and communities to be built around compassion[33]. Which all sounds a lot like something Jesus had to say[34]. Did we see all of that happening? I wish. But we did see some of that happening. No giant leaps but inching forward in a way that brought about mutual change. And where good and God-filled change is happening the Kingdom is breaking through into people's lives. At moments "Your Kingdom come, Your will be done on earth as it is in heaven"[35], becomes more than just a much-loved prayer - it becomes a reality. How amazing is that.

What emerged out of the research and theological thinking we were doing – most people were unaware that it was theological thinking as they tend to think that's for boring old academics and I'm sure working with me confirmed that for them - were 5 core unmet, or partially met, areas where we could contribute. 5 doesn't sound a lot. It is and it remains the same today as there will always be lots of needs, although some of those original core needs have

---

[32] Ann Morisy, Beyond the Good Samaritan, Mowbray 1997 p. 35
[33] David Augsburger, Dissident Discipleship, Brazos Press 2006 pp. 196-7
[34] Luke 4:18-19 (NIV)
[35] Matthew 6:10 (NIV)

changed. Any future involvement would need to be flexible and adapt to socio-economic changes. Some needs move on, some remain, some are beyond the resources and skill set of any church. We are not super-heroes. Leave that to angelic beings.

Looking at those areas where there were gaps in provision it would be easy to think – let's take them all on. That would be a mistake. Attention needs to be paid to the existing resources – both financial and people – the skills and abilities and interests' people have. What is it that people have a real heart for? What is it that they would invest in and believe in? There is always the danger that any church in its enthusiasm and perhaps a little naivety taking on too big a task and ending up failing. We may be about changing the world but one increment at a time seems best. Doing one thing well is better than trying to do 5 and ending up failing. Pinpoint the possible, add faith and courage, and try to deliver something that stands a good chance of being sustainable. There are no certainties but give yourself the best possible chance of success. Later when the provision(s) is established other options can be explored and brought on-line.

All of which meant we developed some existing provisions that the church already had up and running that met a few of the needs that the audit had highlighted for us. This included developing the existing café, the youth provision and restructuring the under 5's programme all of which had been successfully running for years. New provisions included an additional group for young people struggling at school and providing support for schoolwork (aptly called 4-6 as this was the time it ran for – innovative or what?) as well as activities that would help them grow in themselves as young people, and an IT group that would provide support for people struggling to come to terms with the computer age or needing access to computers and wi-fi. All of which required the continuation of the commitment and skills of those already involved in providing provisions accessible for people from the wider community together with new volunteers coming on board with skills relevant to the new provisions.

I'd like to say that we knew what we were doing. Sometimes we did - mostly we didn't. Never let not knowing what you are doing stop you as someone who does will soon join you. Thankfully we had great volunteers who put their heart and soul into making the provision the best it could be and ensured that everyone who accessed the activity felt welcome and valued. And that goes a long way. Setting standards is very important and trying to be professional is too, but at the end of the day warmth and love go a long way. The facilities we had at this point proved more than adequate (thanks to the sacrifice and vision of previous generations) although even then it was clear that in the long term if the project was to develop then we would need to do some seriously thinking about development. That is jumping ahead. More on that later.

I guess that the youth provision was the most challenging. People who were involved at the time still love to tell stories about the things that happened and often are proud to show their scars. Some of them are about the programme that were provided to help these youngsters find their way in life, the trips and activities and the lasting friendships made. Alongside that people who ran their own businesses from the faith community took several of them on as apprentices. So many good things were happening. But there were the fun times too when we developed a very close relationship with the local police who often got called in. Air-gun pellets shot through Ministers windows, fights between young people, young people literally climbing up the wall and entering through an office on the second floor, staff members losing their rag and general mayhem. Today some of those young people, now adults with their own children, are the first to come on site to support events and to keep in touch with those who put their bodies on the line to help them. Many of them have their own businesses and remain true friends to us all. And they always refer to us as 'their church'.

All of which was beginning to have the wonderful knock-on-effect of challenging us all to think about how we were doing church and how the gap between present practices and traditions, and where we were learning people who didn't attend were, might be narrowed. Thankfully, again in my opinion, the gap wasn't so huge that we would have to shut shop and re-open in a new way. Sometimes I wonder if that might be the only solution for some churches. Just saying. We all know that church isn't a building, that church is the gathering of the followers of Jesus, but I have a suspicion we are still a little reticent to widen our understanding too much. Is having in a group of homeless people come into the 'church' building, to be served by people who love Jesus, offered compassion and grace and practical assistance, church? Or does the building have two faces. At times it being used for church, at other times a community centre? Don't we believe that when "two or three gather in my name, there am I with them."[36]. If Jesus is there through the life and witness of the two or three serving and sitting alongside and sharing mutual stories with the clients is that not church? It seems to me that church like a rash (not a nice metaphor but you get my point) is all over the building from Monday to Sunday. In community mission doing church takes on a whole new meaning as I was continuing to discover through my interaction with people from the wider community and helpfully reflected upon through some of those writers who gave fresh theological and practical insight.

Morisy argues that community ministry has a transforming effect on the traditional forms of church ministry such as pastoral care[37]. When a church engages with its community at this level it begins both to make an "assessment" of its struggles and "envisages" a response to them[38]. The point Morisy is making here seems to highlight the necessary movement in the church away from simply 'binding up the broken hearted'[39] (traditional approach to pastoral care) to addressing the causes of the wounds which are often rooted in issues of social justice[40]. When a church is engaging with its community in this way it is moving beyond a limited pastoral response, to a more integrated one which involves the church making a prophetic call for greater social justice through political change. Integrated pastoral care necessitates that the church regains its prophetic voice[41], one that enables it to provide a "prophetic social criticism"[42]. Seemingly for Morisy this happens

---

36 Matthew 18:20 NIV
37 Ann Morisy, Beyond the Good Samaritan, Mowbray 1997 p. 27
38 Ibid p. 28
39 Isaiah 61:1 (NIV)
40 A point developed from: - S.J.Cave, Politicising the Church, M.Th (applied) dissertation, Spurgeons College, London and the University of Wales p. 38
41 Christopher Rowlands, Radical Christianity, Polity Press 1998 pp. 18, 70
42 Christopher Bryant (editor), Restoring faith in Politics, Essay by Norman Shanks, CSM 1996 p. 24

when the community of faith actively engages with the wider community and its needs.

If I have one regret (I'm sure there are many others) I don't think I focussed enough on seeking social justice for those who were clearly being exploited by the 'system'. I note at this point that I'm using the term 'system' because it de-personalises exploitation. Maybe that is why so many writers talk about structures and argue that the demonic is at work in and through them[43]. I don't disagree with them nor with the Apostle Paul when he writes about spiritual warfare engaging "principalities and powers" rather than "flesh and blood"[44]. But the danger in all of that is that it reinforces the idea that exploitation is the result of some hidden force operating in a world beyond our own. In other words, it de-personalises exploitation. What I think I have witnessed over the years is that whilst I agree with all that is being said by others, exploitation is largely channelled through human beings just like me. We did some chasing up, welcomed people on site who had skills in dealing with homelessness, benefits and neglect, engaged local politicians who supported those who clearly where being marginalised and exploited. Just not enough. No theme is mentioned more in the Bible than justice (anything between 400-2000 depending on your interpretation) and in my opinion (here I hold my hand up) no theme is less mentioned in church services.

For Morisy this community-based approach to mission brings the church into the place where it "embraces that wider struggle"[45] for community ministry is about being alongside those who know "the harshness of life"[46]. I couldn't agree more. We saw it daily. I just wish we could have done more to address the conditions of harshness that so many live with daily. So often in community mission the "binding up of wounds"[47] is so overwhelming and is seen as the presenting problem that the causes of the wounds are neglected. That's not an

---

43 For example, John Howard Yoder, The Politics of Jesus, Eerdmans 1972 p.136-138. Note how Yoder links structures with principalities and powers
44 Ephesians 6:12 (NIV)
45 Ann Morisy, Beyond the Good Samaritan, Mowbray 1997 p. 30
46 Ann Morisy, Beyond the Good Samaritan, Mowbray 1997 p. 34
47 Psalm 147:3 (NIV)

excuse just the stark reality of daily engaging with the lives of people. Maybe it is an excuse – you decide but watch out for that plank.

Morisy is keen to point out that involvement in community ministry not only exposes the "brutality and sadness" but the "astonishing dignity" with which people so often meet it[48]. There is no denying it – people are well designed by their Creator. The levels of resilience and human dignity that are to be seen in people living in the most difficult of personal circumstances reflects something of God's image and seeing something of Jesus reflected in them changes assumptions and prejudices. They are not clients, but friends – they are 'us' given a different set of life experiences and circumstances. I think this can help the church move away from focusing on the fallen state of humanity and to reconnect with the image of the creator which is invested in all of humanity[49] (as you will note from the refence below – my idea – one of the few you will find in this book). Morisy stands in a long tradition of Christian Socialists like Ludlow, Maurice and Kingsley[50], who have based their understanding of God's work in the world, and their own response to it, on a high and positive understanding of humanity in relation to God. Maybe not totally my idea then, but without this, the church will struggle to see the possibilities of transformation, and I suspect this paradigm shift in thinking remains a particular challenge for those who identify with an Evangelical tradition[51]. The movement from fallenness to image is central to engaging in community mission and for Morisy this awakening takes place as the church engages in incarnational, community mission. It's certainly an eye opener.

Morisy sees community ministry as the forum for people, both in the Christian community, and those who would place themselves outside it, to "express venturesome love"[52]. Within the context of a church which is taking community ministry seriously there are opportunities for people to participate

---

48 Ann Morisy, Beyond the Good Samaritan, Mowbray, 1997 p. 71
49 A point developed from S.J.Cave, Politicising the Church, M.Th (applied) dissertation, Spurgeons College, London and the University of Wales p. 40
50 John Atherton, Social Christianity A Reader, SPCK 1994 pp. 14-16
51 David K Gillett, Trust and Obey, Darton, Longman and Todd 1993 p. 92
52 Ann Morisy, Journeying Out, Morehouse, 2004 p. 37

in community activity which will provide "transforming experiences"[53] and enable "a story rich life"[54]. In this engagement the community of faith can express its true discipleship by taking the risks that are involved in true care[55]. From the other direction, those who Morisy describes as people who "half-believe"[56], in experiencing involvement that requires venturesome love, are moving onto "stepping stones"[57] that lead towards the worship of God.

On several occasions Morisy refers to what she describes as "deep literacy"[58]. In essence she is referring to the need for people to be able to read their lives in terms of the things that most shape and constrain their lives[59]. The community of faith is not simply there to educate people but to provide opportunities to engage in experiences that will allow for self-education and self-discovery. Central to this is the opportunity to explore faith in the context of venturesome love. Here in this engagement and dialogue, localised theology emerges which is "a situated understanding of the Christian tradition in a particular place at a particular time"[60]. It is this localised theology that emerges out of the dialogue of community ministry that transforms the church and enables spirituality to be integrated with political, social and economic concerns.

Morisy makes some observations on social capital, which she describes as a "new idea" which has emerged from the "arena of social and economic policy"[61] and applies that to community-based mission which creates the opportunity for the church to invest in social capital. There are many different definitions of social capital[62] but the one that seems to fit best with the approach Morisy is taking is provided by Robert Putnam who suggests that, "social capital would facilitate co-operation and mutually supportive relations

---

53 Ibid p. 218
54 Ann Morisy, Journeying Out, Morehouse, 2004 p. 67
55 Ibid p. 204
56 Ann Morisy, Beyond the Good Samaritan, Mowbray 1997 p. 59
57 Ibid p. 59
58 Ibid p. 73
59 Ann Morisy, Beyond the Good Samaritan, Mowbray 1997 p. 73
60 Hans Kung and David Tracy as quoted in John Reader, Local Theology, SPCK 1994 p. 3
61 Ann Morisy, Journeying Out, Morehouse 2004 p. 45
62 http://en.wikipedia.org/wiki/Social_capital

in communities and nations and would therefore be a valuable means of combating many of the social disorders inherent in modern societies, for example crime"[63] (clearly Morisy has been influenced in her thinking by Putnam[64]). This is something that Morisy sees the church investing in through its support for people in need.

However, Morisy challenges the church to avoid what I would describe as a transactional social capital, "I'll do this for you – if you do that for me"[65], and to invest in what I would describe as transformational social capital, "I'll do this for you – without expecting anything in return"[66]. The willingness of the church to make the sacrifices necessary to produce this kind of social capital can have a transformational impact within the community. For Morisy this most involve the willingness on the part of the community of faith to "cross boundaries between strangers"[67]. As the church engages with community issues and their resolution, it is widening not only the trust between the Christian community and the wider community, but also between 'strangers' within the community, to do what Reader describes as making "allies"[68]. This concept is particularly applied to the need for the Christian community to cross the 'boundary of inequality'[69].

---

63 Robert Putman, "Bowling Alone: The Collapse and Revival of American Community", Simon and Schuster 2000
64 Ann Morisy, Journeying Out, Morehouse 2004 p. 48
65 Ibid p. 45
66 Ibid p. 46
67 Ibid p. 45
68 John Reader, Local Theology, SPCK 1994 p. 6
69 Ann Morisy, Journeying Out, Morehouse 2004 p. 217

Chapter 3 – Standing in the Gap

At this time, we were thinking about the way to shape up a social project that would help us engage in community mission. Church based projects broadly speaking didn't have a great reputation for quality and consistency at this time (1996-7). They were often viewed by other community groups and particularly by grant making bodies as 'here today gone tomorrow' and just another way the church was trying to fill empty seats on Sunday's. And no doubt there was truth in that. Thankfully over the years that has changed and many church based social projects have received well deserved plaudits for the excellent contribution they have made to the well-being of many communities. To add to that the Government is always happy for the church to share the burden of social and emotional support with its ready-made body of volunteers. Don't call me cynical.

Given the nature of Baptist Church governance[70] at the time it seemed best for any future social project to be in partnership with the church rather than under the governance of the church so that it could be light on its feet and able to make decisions promptly. Therefore, a project with its own charitable status and board of trustees seemed the obvious direction. It also helped with grant making bodies who particularly at this time were very sceptical about church run social projects. This has changed over the years, as often has church governance, so given a different context a different route might have been taken. At the time this had to be supported and agreed on by the church membership and thankfully it was.

The 'partnership' between the Church and the Project has been central to the growth and well-being of both. We have learnt from each other, and we have

---

70 Traditionally most decisions were made in two/three monthly church members meeting. Today in many Baptist churches decisions are made at various levels by people authorised to do so with the support of the membership. Some Baptist churches no longer have a members meeting opting for an annual AGM.

learnt together. Many have straddled both. At times there has been misunderstandings and inevitably some disagreements. Sometimes it's been the fear that 'the Project has taken over' and at other times 'the Church doesn't support the Project enough'. I'm sure that the feelings behind these statements are real and need to be addressed and over the years we have sought to do that. Not always successfully. I think I could and should have invested more time doing that. Walking a tight rope is never easy and I know I fell off on a few occasions. Thankfully there was always a 'net' of true friends who seemed to grasp the 'project' without ever needing to read a book. I spent hours thinking about the theology behind this (as I have no doubt bored you with all ready), consumed as many books as I could (which allowed me to listen to an awful lot of jazz on YouTube), attended numerous conferences, undertook a Master Degree in Applied theology and later a Doctorate on the relationship of 'faith, politics and spirituality' (still available as an e-book on Amazon – go on you know you want to) – they instinctively grasped the theology and rationale behind community mission. It still annoys me the way God's Spirit does that.

As a team we sat down and began to think about the way we would secure the long-term future of the project. I like to think I'm a bit of a visionary and I could see the direction we needed to travel in but like many visionaries had no clue how that might happen and what would be needed. Thankfully we had people who did. I suspect that one of the greatest crimes churches can commit is to misuse or ignore the talent, experience, and know-how of people in the church. I understand that servanthood is one of the marks of true discipleship but how often do you find someone who heads up a business, runs a school, manages a team in industry, knows how to lay bricks, plaster walls, sort out the plumbing and keep the electricity running, side-roomed into doing something that doesn't touch the sides of their depth of experience.

There can be several reasons for this. Maybe the Minister feels insecure and wants to keep everything under their control so keeps the pool of talent in the pews and uses people whose talents would be best used elsewhere so they can look good and can have a good moan about the people God has given them to work alongside. Maybe it's how people view church. Its quaint, serves a need, doesn't have high expectations of them unlike their working environments. Yet engage them in something that requires their skills and know-how without stripping them of their need for family, leisure, and preparation for work, in time you discover God has provided people who will take a project forward. Trust me gold-dust just lies beneath the surface. Without them there will be no sustainable community mission.

Thankfully we had them. People who understood how to put a business plan together, how to draw up a budget, where income might be sourced, what policies needed to be put into place, how management structures work, how to employ people, draw up contracts, and as we moved forward towards the year 2000 how we might become a recognised charity. Over the long-life of the project so many people have brought their gifting – spiritual gifting – into place and ensured that the project has validity and a good standing in the eyes of community and especially in the view of the charity commissioners. I salute them.

Naming a project, creating a logo, writing a mission statement, setting out goals, raising funds and employing people to manage and run the project are all challenging. Quess which has been the most difficult and sometimes most controversial. Yes, you've got it – a logo! The project name seemed to come very quickly. Closing the gap that exists between a church and its community seemed to be central to what we were setting out to do. So, Gap came easily. But how could we explain it to people who felt there had to be some deeper meaning to it? The idea of an anacronym was mooted. Taking each of the letters it could be – **G**od's **A**ctive **P**resence. It was a great idea but like lots of great ideas it never really caught on. At this point I felt it was time to show my unlimited knowledge of scripture. Having been clueless about most of what was being drawn up and sensing that some of the group where beginning to see me as the 'weakest link' and were getting ready to send me back to the pulpit (what fate can be worse?) I suggested a verse from Ezekiel 22:30 might be a good scriptural base to work out from. "I looked for someone among them who would build up a wall and stand before me in the gap on behalf of the land so I would not destroy it, but I found no-one"[71]. Puffing my chest out I thought, but never said, you all might be able to put a business plan together, but I have knowledge you can only guess at. I could see by the look on their faces that they all knew I had cheated and looked it up before coming to the meeting. Like I cared. So, it was to be the Gap Project – later to avoid a clash with various retail outlets, charities, the London underground and some fine public houses – it became Gap-A Thanet Community Project.

Seriously I love that verse. It captures everything we were about – standing in the Gap – between a people of faith and those who are yet to find faith for themselves. Our desire was to intercede for the community and invite them into the 'atmosphere of the kingdom,' as I love to call it (more of that later). Our yearning to re-build the broken places where people so often live within themselves, such as a lack of a sense of belonging, loneliness, grinding money issues, broken relationships, conditional love, unanswered questions and shattered hopes and dreams. Our heartbeat to discover a people of faith who also share much of that but have found a God who heals and provides hope. "Come and taste (café) and see (our lives as open letters) that God is good; blessed is the one who takes refuge in Him"[72]. And that's it – a people needing refuge meeting a people who have found refuge in God. A community of wounded people meeting a community of wounded people who are discovering that God can heal and restore what is broken – and what is broken is so precious to Him. The café would always be the centre piece that every other activity sparked around. Once people know that Christians love food just as much as they do it breaks down a lot of perceptions and adds a lot of 'weight' to its story. Flinging the doors wide open may also include widening them if the meals the café turn out had anything to do with it.

Now as for the logo. I can help the church to unite around a £2 million project. Give a group of 8 logo choices and the ceiling falls around you. Especially if you had the bright idea of making it into a bit of a competition and families are involved in supporting and campaigning for their own. It was a bad mistake.

---

71 New International Version (NIV)
72 Psalm 34V8 (NIV)

Over the years we have had several logo's and as yet we have never found one that everyone likes. 'Too religious' 'Too childish' 'Too complex' 'Too unreligious' and so it goes on. My advice is finding one on the web and start using it. Who looks at a logo anyway? Famous last words. There are some things that make me glad I'm retired. Logos are way up there.

I remember visibly the first cheque we received to support the project. One of the church members was involved with the Rotary Club and somehow had persuaded them to donate a £1000 towards the project. It was so exciting because it was presented in one of those big cheques that you never get to keep. Photos had to be taken – nothing like a bit of publicity. I still treasure it. My advice to any setting out on a course like this is get into a photo as early as you can. After a while photos can get very crowded and soon you are edged out by others. Some of them didn't even work within the project. It was 'photo bombing' in its infancy. If the project is slow taking off arrange a photo-shoot. You will soon have a crowd.

I remember the 'bridge' illustration from my college days. The picture is of a bridge that the church is building towards the community but simply waiting for people to come across and join them. There are a lot of near empty churches still waiting – we all know it's not going to happen. So, the idea the tutors were trying to convey is that the church must get over the bridge and find ways of connecting with people and accompanying them back over the bridge. I think at first, I thought this meant escorting people (sometimes in hand-cuffs – often by lulling them into a false sense of security) over the bridge into the church. Thankfully somehow a small light bulb was switched on in my head. I soon realised that for me the bridge is the bridge to faith not necessarily to the church – a small disagreement with some wonderful and respected teachers – although its joyful when people come and join the community of faith. The priority of the faith community is to introduce people to Jesus.

When people ask questions about the ethos of community mission one of their burning issues is 'how many people have joined your church through it?'.

Normally it's because they are not experiencing church growth themselves and, being kind, would like to know how that might happen. Being unkind they simply want to 'poo poo' the whole idea of community mission as defunct and failing mission. Unscriptural and unfaithful even. I don't know how many people have joined the church since we set out – seldom do people come to church for anyone single reason or means, but we have seen church growth. Community Mission as I understand it and have sought to practice it is about giving people the opportunity to meet and follow Jesus. They may well decide to express that in non-traditional ways (whatever that might be) but my understanding, indeed conviction is, that its Jesus that saves and not the church. Correct me if I'm wrong. Basically, what I'm trying to say is that I personally never set out to increase church numbers but to introduce people to the most amazing Saviour. I guess many have become part of the church community and I thank God for that. More importantly is have they found Jesus? Don't set out on community mission if its main purpose is to fill the seats on Sunday. You may well be disappointed. We are here to support the building of the kingdom of which the church is one visible component but not the whole shooting match. If that's not a case of mixed or possibly inappropriate metaphors my levels of sensitivity are failing. I like it though, so it stays in.

One of the criticisms of the way we have set about community mission is that it's all 'in-house'. I get that as that's how it can seem. Through the resources we provide for people they come on site (in large numbers). I think where those who have been critical – and criticism is no bad thing nor unwelcome if it makes you think and is meant well (and generally most of it was) – have missed a trick with the model we have sought to build. Hold your breath – the building hosts two communities. One is the 'in-house' community of faith and the other is 'out of house' people who have not yet discovered faith but could do so. The bringing together of two groups of people in different places regarding faith and sharing life in the same building. What could possibly go wrong?

My vision was to be able to walk out of the door of my office (mainly shared with other squatters – I think they call it 'hot desking') and into the wider community. Crossing the smallest bridge in the world and out into the community. Whilst spiritually a gap may well remain between the two communities at least it saves on petrol or shoe leather. Within metres I could have a conversation with someone from the wider community. That was the cunning plan. That is not to say that I wasn't involved outside the building, nor would I encourage others not to be. Weddings (off site), funerals of people from the wider community, hospital visits, care homes, schools and so on, some weekly or monthly. That was just in my role as a Minister. Not to mention restaurants, pubs, sport venues, jazz clubs and various unmentionable locations which I hope no-one checks the CCTV. I'm not saying that this model is for everybody it was just for us. Others have other models and callings. That's just as good, maybe they would say better.

Many of our faith community are involved in all kinds of community activities outside the building and seldom if ever apart from a Sunday would come on-site and we celebrate that. I wish I had made more of it. I think we tried but not often enough. People need affirming in their role outside the community of faith whether in a paid or voluntary capacity as an equal calling. It's all too easy for the church to project the image that it's only those who are working within its boundaries that are the 'chosen one's' who always get to read at the 'Carols by Candlelight' service.

Chapter 4 – A Charitable Enterprise

On January 19th 2001 the Gap Project was formally registered with the Charity Commission. All the hard work to achieve this goal was carried out by the Steering Group and I provided the biscuits. When we talk about a willingness to pay the 'cost' in discipleship I had no idea that this would include so many biscuits. Over the time I had to lower the crossbar from Chocolate Hob-nobs to Rich-Tea, but never once did I resort to Fig-Biscuits. We needed no further stimulation to keep us running. Still 'an army marches on its stomach'[73] and we munched our way through the process. A process that had taken four years to formalise. The 'Unincorporated Association' document had been drawn up previously in September 2000 and took three months to be accepted which given the workload of the charity Commission was impressive.

Most of the Constitution was laid out by the pro-forma provided by the Charity Commission itself. What created the biggest discussion was how we would define the Project in terms that conveyed our Christian faith but also our desire for the Project to be inclusive and accessible to all. If funders were to be attracted, it was important that we allayed their concerns that this Project wouldn't be overtly 'Evangelistic' but at the same time uphold the integrity of Christian faith and the church which stood in partnership with it, and I was one of the Ministers of. At times it felt a little like a 'tightrope' walk but we were determined to cross it. In the end this is how it was written.

To run a community project which will promote and further the well-being and quality of life, relieve poverty where possible, improve family relationships and advance educational opportunities of a wide age range of people, particularly the disadvantaged and vulnerable in the Thanet community.

---

73 Apparently attributed to both Napoleon and Federick the Great

It is based on Christian principles, non-judgemental and holistic in its purposes.

In these objects it seeks to work with other agencies, both statutory and voluntary.

Would it be written differently in 2024? I'm not sure. It certainly has stood the test of time. Is it true to the ethos of 'Community Mission'? You can be the judge of that as we have looked at the theology that underpins this approach to bringing church and community into relationship. In 2000 it seemed to be the right label which hopefully did and continues to do what it says on the can.

One of the initial conversations we needed to have both in the Project and in the Church was about National Lottery Funding. Introduced in 1994 there were lots of different opinions expressed ranging from it being guilty of exploiting the poorest and most vulnerable in society to an important and much needed resource for 'good causes'. At the time the Project was developing, lots of charities were applying for funding from the National Lottery Fund and securing sizable amounts which often stabilised the future for at least another year. Naturally in the Church there was a lot of debate about the ethics of the National Lottery and whether Church either individually or collectively should apply to it for financial support. Initially in both the Church and the Project there was an aversion to applying directly to the Fund for support.

Over the years I think that view somewhat mellowed as it became increasingly difficult to apply to any funder for support without the funder itself having first received Lottery money. I must confess I did rather turn a blind eye to applications made to funders who were passing on money received from the Lottery. It was either that or staff kept quiet about it, and I never asked. No harm in a bit of ignorance. I'm not adverse to having a little bit of wool pulled over my eyes when it means people's lives can be improved. In truth though I have always been on the side of those who argued that Nehemiah used the Kings money to aid and support his enterprise of returning to Jerusalem and restoring the walls and city life[74]. The Kings money would have been 'tainted' by conquest and the subjugation of foreign nations. It seems to me then that finance that possibly comes from a source that as a Christian you are not totally in favour of can be used to support and bless a community where many people have needs. The other day I walked past a local church which proudly displayed a sign stating that it is supported by the National Lottery Fund. So far as I could see no lightning bolt had taken out its roof – and I suspect it is the roof that's being funded. So far so good. Like the sign shows keep your fingers crossed though. Just in case.

Naturally everyone must work through that individually given their own context and convictions, but I personally support the idea of 'redeeming' money for the sake of kingdom enterprise. Naturally there must be limits on that and there are obvious examples which I could not agree with. Any funding with so many strings attached to it that it takes aware the integrity, independence and ethos of a Project would be included in that. As would any support from a football team and rugby club I didn't support. Even I have standards. I must confess though when individuals in the church have asked me whether they should be buying Lottery tickets I have always told them to not let anyone know if they win and then tithe it secretly. Maybe I didn't have standards just projects that need funding.

One of the Ministers of the church at Queens Road plays the role of an 'ex-officio trustee' which is embedded in the Gap Constitution and has the joy as well as the challenge of bridging both. Together with that we have always tried to ensure that the majority of Gap Trustees are not only 'in sympathy with the Christian ethos of the Project[75]' but a committed and regular part of the life of the Church. Again, with this we have wanted the 'team leaders' of the various activities that make up the Project to be the same. As well as aiding the partnership of Project and Church this has the added advantage of avoiding that 'tipping point' that projects face when most of the key players in a project have

---

[74] Nehemiah 2:7-9 NIV
[75] As stated in the Gap Project Constitution as the basis for any person seeking a paid or voluntary role its activities

little or no connection with either faith or the partner church. I have seen projects reach that point and how that has led to a break-down in relationship between the host church and the social project. Involving people from the wider community in a church-based project is an absolute must as we will go on to see – abdicating overall control of its direction in my opinion will create problems that will affect both project and church.

Raising the funding that would be needed to support a growing project would always be a challenge. Here I want to pay tribute to the many staff at the Gap Project who spent hours and hours applying for funding from grant makers. Big charities pay large salaries to fund-raisers – we paid small salaries, and they made big gains for the project. Such was their commitment. There were times, and I'm sure there remain times, when the funding didn't seem to be coming in. At the Executive Meetings financial updates would be given and the situation looked dire. Thankfully the Executive Committee remained steadfast and resisted the temptation of making cuts that would hinder the development of the project and the work it was engaged in. The church acting as the partner charity was generous and always supportive and we sensed that the churches investment in community mission would not ultimately be allowed to simply die. The project was able to invest in resources that greatly benefitted and enhanced the work of the church. It was a partnership with both mutual commitment and benefit. I cannot express too strongly the need for the host church and the project to believe in each other and remain committed to its gaol of community mission. To have as many people as possible that are investing in both. At times the church struggled financially with its commitment to staffing and the future development of the on-site facilities and the project was able to off-set that through paying rent for the use of the facilities together with its investment in shared resources and staff that were based in the building during the week. Having one of the Ministers straddling both church and project helped, and a number of the Executive Committee always played significant leadership roles in the church. Having witnessed the sad demise of local church-based projects I cannot express too many times how vital that relationship is. Looking back, I know that I failed to bring the Executive Committee and the staff and volunteers of the project together with church leaders as much as I should have done. We did have one or two joint gathering looking at mutual and shared vision, but it was not enough. Don't make the same mistake.

It was clear from the early days of the project that for it to develop in the way it hoped we would need both paid staff as well as paid sessional workers. Like all things it would not happen overnight, and our first break came when we secured a back to work scheme that paid the princely sum of £25 a week. This meant we could advertise for a project manager. Following on from someone taking that role on a short-term basis the first long-term project manager responded to the opportunity. To be honest we couldn't believe our good fortune. Someone who had been a social worker, highly qualified, and having been out of paid employment to support a family business and bring up a family was standing at our door asking if she would fit the role. Clearly it wasn't the salary that attracted her to the project. Not only did she have all the skills and personality we were looking for but also clearly grasped the ethos of the project as an expression of community mission. Sometimes 'gold-dust' comes knocking at your door. Maybe we got lucky maybe it was meant to be. For me it was like the seal of God's favour upon all that we had together been doing. She would prove to be Gap's first long-term project manager and only retired in 2023. Her involvement would set the project alight, and I could take a side-ways step and support in a different way. I cannot tell you how vital it is to any project to have the right person heading it up. God brought us the right person and although I'm doing the writing here, I know that without her there would be no story to tell.

Alongside this. Gap has been able to provide additional levels of management – people who have worked together with the Project manager with a particular area of oversight. All have brought much to the project and have been essential to the way the project has continued to evolve over the years. With the impending retirement of the longtime serving project manager this has provided a sense of continuity which I believe ensures a bright future for the project. The project is in good hands. We were fortunate to be able to employ people in this way and it provided good transition and succession. This is always for the well-being of a project particularly if people have worked over a long period of time.

Over the years of the project, we have been able to employ several key staff. All of them have proved indispensable. Some have stayed and others have moved on. The café which was at the heart of the project was able to employ staff and expand from 1 day a week to 5 and then to 6. Providing good value for money and a place to be, has helped grow the project in so many ways. Often, it's the first resource that people from the community make use of. Finding a welcome, warmth, friendship, and good quality food often leads to them becoming part of some of the other activities the project offers. Sometimes they make it to church as they sense the 'atmosphere of the kingdom' which underpins all that makes the project distinctive. The involvement of people with 'additional needs' as volunteers in the café has been invaluable and the café would not function without them. It often requires an investment of time from the café staff, but the mutual benefits make it worthwhile.

Employing a team leader for the under-fives project, securing an amazing team of sessional workers, has provided support for young families that is highly valued by the wider community. Not only is there a commitment to high standards and meaningful educational activities but a bucket load of love and concern. Over the years the range of activities has expanded and now includes alongside the normal parent and toddler and pre-nursery groups, support for first-time parents as well as parents with 'down-syndrome' babies. It truly is a beautiful thing and again its success is down to the commitment of the team. As a spin-off from this family café was established where Christian faith can be shared in a relaxed but more open way.

The project in partnership with the church has been able to provide a dedicated children's and youth worker. At first this was a shared commitment between church and project but more recently taken on by the church. Several people over the years have played a part in the development of this role. Youth culture moves breathtakingly fast, and the project side of youth work has had to adapt. Seemingly the days of running open youth clubs has become too difficult to manage so smaller more invitational groups have been tried. Some of this has proved long-lasting whilst others have moved away. Naturally the church wants to develop programmes that are aimed at their own young people and welcome immediate friends who come with them. As a result, there is a strong church-based group lead by an amazing team and a gifted children's and youth worker. It is wonderful to see. One of my regrets – where I could have done more – is that a youth provision for young people from the community has mainly slipped away. It was one of the original core needs that the audit highlighted and I would suggest remains a need. If I am to be self-critical, I think I could have tried harder to maintain and support a youth provision for young people from the wider community or at least got involved with such a provision that others are working at elsewhere. Now I suspect I'm far too old and my technological know-how runs out around 2005. It was always edgy work, and I think somewhere along the line some of my edginess got smoothed over. It happens. Don't neglect the 'edgy' it's where the fun is.

Mainly run by volunteers with one or two sessional workers Gap developed an educational programme. Right from the outset of the project the need for IT training and support became obvious. So many people, particularly seniors were being left behind by the technological revolution taking place. Alongside the one-to-one tutoring in the designated IT room, Gap was able to set up College courses that were linked into the weekly programme. This has proved a great resource for the community and the provision is now offered twice a week. The quality and commitment of the voluntary team never fails to impress, and all served up with a large dose of humour. Together with this a numeracy and literacy group meet weekly. Run by a sessional worker together with a team of volunteers it has provided much needed support and educative value to a wide group.

Having now reached the age when I qualify for the senior activities I register a personal interest here. Looking back over the last few years one of the memories that remain is of the members of the senior group returning after the easing of restrictions following the pandemic. You did not need to be a psychologist to see the cost of that time of isolation and anxiety etched on their faces. But walking into the building, being together again, taking up the activities on offer, laughing and joking as they returned to the 'sit and be fit' programme was priceless. After a while the years seemed to fall away, melted under the sheer joy of being part of a community of friends. Over the two years of varied but telling restrictions, the team that head up this area of the project had selflessly found ways to continue to support and to keep in contact with this age group. It truly was a beautiful thing, and the rewards were there to see as friendships were renewed. Never underestimate the power and importance of supporting seniors and providing community for those who often spend too many days alone. It's an investment which I hope to cash in on one day.

Providing a resource for people who for all kinds of reasons have found themselves homeless or housed in properties that lack facilities and where the environment can often be intimidating was always going to be a challenge. However, support for some of the most vulnerable and unpredictable was crucial to a project that was seeking to support need in the widest sense within the community. Being realistic about what we could provide and partnering with others who could provide more and offer greater expertise gave the resource a sense of partnership. For Gap it was the provision of a good meal, access to the phone, advice on how to connect with the other agencies who offered much more than Gap could, and later when we moved into the new building somewhere for laundry to be done and a hot shower taken. A cupboard of donated clothes and new underwear helped. Inevitably this provision was always going to be 'edgy' and not everyone who volunteered continued, sometimes inbuilt attitudes towards vulnerable and demanding people came to the fore and gently people had to encouraged into volunteering in another area of the project where they would be better used. There is no shame in any of that.

Dealing with people with addictions, mental-health issues and unstructured lives can be very demanding. Sometimes the afternoon much to everyone's relief would pass without incident. Sometimes all hell would break loose, and fists and chairs would fly everywhere. Learning to duck, to not look intimidated when someone is threatening you with a bottle of drink – you know that they won't smash it over your head unless its empty – how to try to calm the situation when inside you are anything but calm. Yet amid all that a deep sense that its worthwhile. Over the years friendships have been made which are valued by all those involved in helping to support this resource. Sometimes people just want some quiet and for you to pray with them. Occasionally and tragically, you lose one the friends you have made – robbed of life by relentless and destructive addictions. Sometimes you get to hold a memorial service for them and at other times to attend their funerals. They will never ignore you in the street and sometimes when you sit alongside them at a bus-stop where they will sleep the night you share a moment of common humanity, and you see something of the image of God in them.

Thanet is an area where over the years people with additional needs have been provided for. Sometimes in schools with accommodation, often in homes where they can live and flourish with support, and more recently served by schools but living with their families. Not only has Gap benefitted from the hard work and skills of those who volunteer in the café but been able to provide various groups to support the excellent work going on in the wider community including a 'youth club' a couple of times a month called WEB (welcome everybody). Several spin offs from that have evolved over the years providing the opportunity for them to explore the Christian faith. Recently a support group for parents with down-syndrome babies was started. I can't imagine how big the smile that has put on God's face, but I can see the smile on the faces of the parents and all these amazing children, young people and young adults that have found a home in the building. If I ever feel 'low' or want to moan about how my life is I know where to go and soon the smile is back. They are truly inspirational and always know when things aren't quite right for you. Ten minutes with them and the light is back on.

Much has been written about the increase in the number of people of all ages and backgrounds suffering mental-health issue. Gap has responded in several ways including a weekly 'well-being café'. What started out as a small intimate group grew quickly which reflects the need for people to be able to find support and togetherness and the healing that can bring. Included in the afternoon is the opportunity if they chose to join in with a reflective group which gathers in the chapel (on site). It's a simple but deeply profound sharing of Christian faith and God's commitment to the well-being and wholeness of all people. Having said that I suspect it's the bingo and the quizzes that really draws people in. They are a lot of fun.

What began as a project aimed at off-setting 5 core needs in the community of 2001 has evolved over the year and remains relevant to a community of shifting needs. Challenges remain but the project has remained steadfast to its ethos and calling. People have come and gone – some remain – but each one through their lives and commitment to this expression of community mission has made the difference. If there are three things that make a project successful it would firstly be people, secondly people and lastly people. And of God in people. It's a winning formula.

Chapter 5 – A new building

On June 11th, 2011, over 1100 people came to celebrate the opening of the new building at Queens Road Baptist Church. The day was filled with different activities and culminated in one amazing worship service. The project and the church had moved off-site for 18 months and even though the building we hired was limited in space there was a determination to keep all the provisions provided by the project up and running which was largely successful. The project team were simply amazing, and everyone made the best of limited space and facilities. I suspect the both the project, and the church came out of the experience stronger than when they first moved off-site.

Maintaining a sense of continuity with those who had sacrificially enabled the project and church to thrive prior to 2009 the new building both honours and reflects their commitment. Not only in its physical design but in its DNA. Having spent a few years building models out of 'Lego' or playdough in the end it was the experts who designed the existing building blending old with new in a seamless manner. The building committee, finance committee and fabric committee were visionary and laboured endlessly towards the goal. Every now and again when their skill set fell short, they looked to me to get more biscuits which fuelled the whole process. If ever there was a project and new building fuelled by biscuits this was it. Money was raised within the church and thanks to a lot of hard work and endeavour a loan for £1m from the Baptist Union was obtained and a project costing £2m was began. I still don't understand how all that money came in but then I don't understand how my pocket money is worked out weekly. It did and the loan is almost paid off. By the time you are reading this it may well be paid-off which means I can ask for expenses for the mountain of biscuits I have bought since 1996. Don't hold your breath – I won't.

In this context what can I say about the new building? At a personal level I guess it taught me to not give up on your vision. I hasten to add a shared vision with so many. The process of arriving at a decision to go forward with the new building was not straight forward. The first time we as a leadership team took the concept to the church meeting it fell-just short on the 90% we had looked for. Having "rendered my garments and poured ash all over my head",[76] sat in a darkened room sucking my thumb for a period, I realised that the Prophet Joel was right. I needed to assure that my 'heart' was right before God and the church. Sometimes church leaders can get carried along by their visions and miss out on the need to take people with them especially caring for those who for a whole load of different and genuine reasons are finding it difficult to get onboard with the vision. The next few months were busy and lots of conversations happened. I was determined to carry those who found the building project too difficult with us. I think I mostly did that but then I am an optimist. Whatever they were very kind and generous, and no death threats were received. Seriously they were gracious, and I can't tell you how much that means. We took a new proposal to the church meeting nine months later and it was supported.

The existing facilities at Queens Road were very adequate for the project up to 2009 but it became clear if the project (and indeed the church) were to continue to develop in the way we hoped new facilities would be needed. The new building was designed around a vision for where we wanted to go and mostly that has been fulfilled. No one building can provide everything you need (want) but it is one amazing place and it's a joy to walk through its doors. Shower facilities for the homeless, or those who's facilities at home no longer can be safely used, a designated IT suite, a chapel (sacred space) for common use, offices for staff, a purpose built café and kitchen, lots of rooms for various activities being used by both the church community and the wider community, an attic space designated for young people and a auditorium which is big enough to fit an air-craft carrier in. Slight exaggeration there. The ethos we pursued was that we would not be precious about any of the spaces. They would be shared space; multi-purpose and the community would see it as theirs as much as it was ours. Over the years hiring the facilities to various community groups has not only provided a necessary income for the church to

---

[76] Joel 2:13 (NIV)

maintain its mission but we have made so many friends in the process. Today well over 1000 people enter the building every week and access the various resources we have made available to them.

To enable community mission to happen several different approaches have been taken. At one point the church appointed chaplains to each of the activities which had some success, many of the activities have or continue to have opportunities for people to explore Christian faith, weekly devotions take place which volunteers can attend should they chose, but in the end its those who live out their Christian faith in a natural and grounded way that have made the greatest impact. Currently (2023) the church has asked one of the Ministers to focus on the weekly activities of the project and to get alongside people daily. Now that's what I call a great vision. I can't wait to see how that is going to work out. Love a bit of community mission.

Like all projects Gap has lived at times 'hand to mouth'. Funding is and always has been since inception a challenge. Developing some kind of social enterprise to help support the project became more of a necessity as time went on. Whilst the café does provide a source of income profits are marginal as the emphasis has always been on providing good quality food at affordable prices. People sometimes pay a small amount for the various resources they receive but it remains just that – a small amount – and long may that remain the case. The greater source of sustainable income has come from the setting up of a charity shop – known as 'Gap in the market' – in the high street. It was a big enterprise to take on and whilst it took a few years to find its feet, today it provides significant funding for the project. Managed brilliantly, supported by an excellent team of volunteers it has made a huge contribution to community life in Broadstairs. It is valued by the Executive Committee and staff of the Gap Project. Check it out if you are in the High Street of Broadstairs anytime.

Not only does the project fulfil its responsibilities to the Charity Commissioners but as part of its constitution holds an annual general meeting (AGM). Whilst there are always business matters that must be dealt with the greater emphasis is on 'storytelling'. People can tell something of their own story and how the project has supported them. It's a powerful and moving time and ensures that the project always focusses on what is most important and the rationale for its existence. Storytelling is often at the heart of the church. Traditionally known as giving a 'testimony' it has shaped its telling around certain expectations. Almost always there needs to be some reference to personal conversion – a life changing encounter with Jesus. The more dramatic the better. Nothing wrong with that I hear you say, and you are right. But people encounter Jesus in different ways and not in some prescribed manner. Story telling in the post-modern society too is valued very highly and that is often reflected through the way the media deliver news. It's a powerful medium and over the years the AGM has provided examples of that. Maybe the stories need to be heard more often as they provide inspiration and a sense of direction. Maybe they need to be heard in church too or is that too risky and if it is why? Jesus spent a lot of time listening to stories that for many churches would be perceived to be unorthodox[77].

Ann Morisy sees that as supporting people to have "story-rich lives"[78] Possibly today too many people have "story thin lives"[79]. There can be no doubt that community mission as expressed in a project such as it is here, can help people to enrich their personal stories and that can have 'faith outcomes'. Morisy sees that in terms of people being continuously shaped by their stories, which in turn inform the choices they make and give them new direction for their lives[80]. This has benefit both for those who already hold a Christian faith – as they are involved in community mission so their stories become enriched by their experiences – and those exploring faith whose story can help re-orientate the church as it engages in community mission. It's a win-win. And who can resist a win-win. Not me for sure.

---

77 Mark 5:25-34 (NIV)
78 Ann Morisy, Journeying Out, Morehouse 2004 p. 67
79 Ibid p. 79
80 Ibid pp. 70-71

Recommended Reading

Augsburger, D. (2006), *Dissident Discipleship*, Barzos Press

Chalke, S. (2004), *Trust*, Authentic

Dorr, D. (1984), *Spirituality and Justice*, Gill and Macmillan

Duncan, M. (2006), *Building a Better World*, Continuum

Gillett, D. (1993), *Trust and Obey*, Darton, Longman and Todd

Hauerwas, S. (1991), *After Christendom*, Abingdon Press

Hauerwas, S. (1981), *A Community of Character*, University of Notre Dame Press

Leech, K. (1981), *The Social God*, Sheldon Press

Leech, K. (1988), *Struggle in Babylon*, Sheldon Press

Leech, K. (1990), *Care and Conflict*, Darton, Longman and Todd

Leech, K. (1992), *The Eye Of The Storm*, Darton Longman and Todd

Leech, K. (1994), *Soul Friend*, Darton Longman and Todd

Leech, K. (1997), *The Sky is Red*, Darton Longman and Todd

Leech, K. (2001), *Through Our Long Exile*, Darton, Longman and Todd

Morisy, A. (1997), *Beyond the Good Samaritan*, Mowbray

Morisy, A. (2004), *Journeying Out*, Morehouse

Morisy. A (2009), *Bothered and Bewildered*, Continuum

Reader, J. (1994), *Local Theology*, SPCK

Wallis, J. (1981), *The Call to Conversion*, Lion Paperback

Wallis, J. (1994), *The Soul of Politics*, Orbis Books

Wallis, J. (2000), *Faith Works*, SPCK

Wallis, J. (1987), (ed), *The Rise of Christian Conscience*, Harper and Row

Yoder, J. (1964), *Discipleship as Political Responsibility*, Herald Press

Yoder, J. (1992), *Body Politics*, Discipleship Resources

Yoder, J. (1964), *The Christian Witness to the State*, Herald Press

www.ingramcontent.com/pod-product-compliance
Lightning Source LLC
Chambersburg PA
CBHW061225070526
44584CB00029B/3996